A Survivor's Story

My Story of Survival from Domestic Violence

Yvonne Davis-Weir

WESTBOW
P R E S S®
A DIVISION OF THOMAS NELSON
& ZONDERVAN

Scripture taken from the King James Version of the Bible.

WestBow Press books may be ordered through booksellers or by contacting:

WestBow Press
A Division of Thomas Nelson & Zondervan
1663 Liberty Drive
Bloomington, IN 47403
www.westbowpress.com
1 (866) 928-1240

ISBN: 978-1-5127-1640-5 (sc)
ISBN: 978-1-5127-1641-2 (hc)
ISBN: 978-1-5127-1639-9 (e)

Library of Congress Control Number: 2015916995

Print information available on the last page.

WestBow Press rev. date: 10/23/2015

Contents

Preface

Writing about the issue of domestic violence, or any kind of violence is never easy. Even though it is something that seemed better left untouched, however it must be publicized, because many people are experiencing it every day. I love to write, but this was the hardest, and most painful issue I ever had to write about. As a survivor of domestic violence, I was determined to bury that part of my life forever, never to be mentioned again. This is an embarrassing topic that no one enjoy talking about. I thought that by covering it up it would eventually disappear. I thought I was home free for over twenty years, until that part of my life was aroused, and I realized that I have a duty to help others by telling my story. As a pastor I realize that there are many people today who are living in domestic abusive situations. They refuse to talk about it because they are either ashamed, or they may think that no one will believe, or listen to them. There are also many church goers today who are silently living in this violent lifestyles. My prayer is that this book will give others the courage to break their silence and speak up against this ugly issue. By doing so, many lives can be saved. "Domestic violence, or intimate partner violence, affects millions of women and men each year. It may include physical abuse, sexual abuse, threat of physical or sexual abuse and emotional abuse" (Chapman, G., 2008, p.135).

After reading this book, I pray that you will be determined to break your silence by seeking the help you need so that you can live your life to its fullest. For those who are mothers or fathers, it's all the more important to address the issue, because your children must be raised with the understanding that violence of any kind is not okay. For those victims who are not parents, you also bear the responsibility to enlighten others about the dangers of domestic violence. So no matter who we are or where we are from, we all have the obligation to share our experience with others.

My regret is that I did not come forward sooner, so the number of those who suffered or probably died would have been lessened. Now I am on a mission to let victims know that help is available, and they don't have to live their lives as someone else's prey.

For those who are survivors, I am appealing to you to join me in this fight for the common purpose of reducing the numbers of domestic abusers. I agree that it is impossible to save everyone but for every victim reached means one more family saved.

The Lord inspired His faithful people to write these words in the Bible to show how much He loves and cares:

1 Peter 3:7 says " Likewise, ye husbands, dwell with them according to knowledge, giving honour unto the wife, as unto the weaker vessel, and as being heirs together of the grace of life; that your prayers be not hindered" (KJV).

Galatians 5:19-21 "Now the works of the flesh are manifest, which are these; Adultery, fornication, uncleanness, lasciviousness, Idolatry, witchcraft, hatred, variance, emulations, wrath, strife, seditions, heresies, Envyings, murders, drunkenness, revellings, and such like: of the which I tell you before, as I have also told you in time past, that they which do such things shall not inherit the kingdom of God" (KJV).

Luke 4:18-19 also says The Spirit of the Lord is upon me, because he hath anointed me to preach the gospel to the poor; he hath sent me to heal the brokenhearted, to preach deliverance to the captives, and recovering of sight to the blind, to set at liberty them that are bruised, To preach the acceptable year of the Lord" KJIV). Jesus' main purpose was to heal the broken-hearted like you and I, and to free us from the captivity of physical violence.

Acknowledgment

It pleases me to acknowledge one of my favorite persons, Dr. Patricia Colangelo, one of the great professors at Trinity International University in Davie, Florida. It was because of her influence why I was able to write this book. It is now because of her, many probably thousands of people who are living with violence will be helped. This was a part of my life which I was never proud of, and as a result, I attempted to conceal it every way I could. During several sessions in her class, I began to understand the urgency and importance of sharing my experience with others. Thanks to her, many will know that they too can escape the hurt of domestic violence. Thank you, Professor Colangelo.

My Prayer for Strength

My Father in Heaven, as I am getting ready to write this book, I am asking you for the strength needed to get the information to others who are suffering from domestic abuse. As I am writing I am shaking and feeling very nervous, so Lord please help me in this effort. I never dreamed of writing this book because I wanted to keep everything a secret because of embarrassment. Lord please give me the spirit of boldness as I awaken this part of my life that I am not proud of. Help me to understand that by doing so, many people will be helped as a result. I thank You Lord for leading me in this direction. I thank You for strengthening me, and giving me the courage to write. I love You Lord, amen.

CHAPTER ONE

My Journey Began

Coming from a small island to this wonderful country, a land of many opportunities, and being a few years out of high school, I thought I hit the jackpot. I thought that my childhood dreams has finally come through. In fact I thought I was the luckiest girl in the world, because I married the man of my dreams, my high school sweetheart and was looking forward (as the fairy tale story said) living happily ever after. I felt like Cinderella marring her Prince Charming and riding off into the sunset and living happily after.

As a child growing up in the island, I used to hear so many wonderful things about this great country, which someone once described to me as 'heaven'. I often wondered what life would be like living here. I remembered wondering if this was a place where people actually walked on the ground. I once heard one of my neighbors asking if there was actually dirt in this 'enchanted' country.

So, when the occasion arose for me to travel, I was happy because I looked at it as a chance at happiness, plus an opportunity to help my parents who struggled to keep me in school over the years. Therefore, as a high school graduate who was pursuing nursing, I jumped at the offer to fulfill my dreams to care for my family. My high school sweetheart and I were married and I began my journey to another part of the world, a place of many opportunities. Traveling to this country was a wonderful experience, but little did I know the horror I would later endure.

I arrived here with my husband and our son then three years old, feeling very excited because I believed that this was my chance at happiness as well as an opportunity for me to get a better education. Settling down was a bit challenging because I was thrust into a new life as a wife, and in a whole new culture, far different from what I was accustomed. However I tried to enjoy everything one day at a time. I thought to myself that as time goes by, everything would work out and I would be the happiest person in the world. I firmly believed that if I exercise patience a little longer, everything will become magical and wonderful.

Things were going quite well as I expected and I was very happy, however after a while I took off my rose-colored glasses and I began to see things as they really were. For a long time I managed to fight back by erasing the things that didn't fit with my fairy tale lifestyle. Instead I held on to the thought that nothing would interfere with my enchanted world. As a matter of fact I decided that no matter what happened, I must do what's necessary to ensure that the unity and happiness of my family stayed intact, by any means, even if it hurts me. However, I later realized that no matter how hard I tried to hold on to the things that were not earnest and wholehearted, eventually I must let go. Getting out of the situation was important (as much as I didn't want to) for me to retain my sanity and build upon the little self-esteem I had left.

After a few years, life in this 'heaven' that I dreamed about became such a misery, a nightmare. It was so bad that I wished to be back home, I was no longer impressed. (I must set the record straight by saying that this wonderful country has been very good to me with its many, many opportunities. It has so much to offer, of which I am very grateful. Migrating to this place had nothing to do with the torture I endured). As said previously, the thrill and excitement disappeared, nothing enticed me anymore. I longed to be back home where there was very little resources, not much money; but there was love, and lots of it. I began to miss the little things I used to take for granted over the years. The things which seemed to be annoying to me then, I yearned for them, I wanted them back. Included are appreciating my family and friends, listening to the roosters crowing in the early morning hours (our alarm clocks). It irritated me then, but somehow I missed hearing them. Also hearing my dad trying to round up his squealing pigs very early in the mornings. I also missed hearing my mom fighting with the hens to steal their eggs from their nests so she could prepare breakfast for the family. I also missed hearing my neighbors yodeling across the hill as they converse back and forth. I used to pull the covers over my head, which didn't help much. All these things I overlooked over the years, which annoyed me then, I longed for them, I yearned for them. Clayton Howell says, "There was no money to buy groceries. We were poor because there was no money to buy material things as we know them today. Being raised poor is a hard life. Love of family for one another make it all worthwhile though" (Howell, 2011, p. 14). That was exactly how I felt then, nothing else mattered to me except to get back on the plane. As a result, all the excitement of being here subsequently faded away and I wanted to return and return to my 'country' life of living. It wasn't easy being in a foreign country with no family (except my husband and my son), and very little chance of seeing my parents and sisters again, at least not for a long time.

It happened that my fear became a reality about a year later when my dad passed away. I thought to myself 'this couldn't be happening', 'I didn't get to tell him that I loved him', 'I didn't get the chance to repay him'. I kept saying 'something's wrong; this is not how it was supposed to be.' It took a toll on me, so bad that I became disheartened. Then I began to be concerned about my mother, and wondered if I would be able to see her again. My initial goal was to repay my parents for the sacrifices they made to keep me in school over the years, to care for them the way I wanted. The passing of my dad was very devastating, and made wanting to return home even more to be with my mom.

> How we respond to any given psychological stress is entirely up to us, which by itself is a huge problem. It takes an enormous degree of character to choose to be responsible for all that occurs in your life and to realize that even if you can't control all of the events, you can control how you feel about it (Weinstein, R., 2004, n.p).

In our culture, we are not on the affectionate side; habitual appreciation is not something we expressed every day, we just know that we are loved. We never actually sat down to have heart-to-heart talks like I do now with my children. We hardly hugged, but strangely enough we felt the love. There were hardly ever any 'I love you's' growing up in my home. The affections were shown only in deeds, not in words; nothing was expressed verbally because these expressions of love and affection were expected of us. Nevertheless we somehow felt loved and protected – it is somewhat hard to explain but I hope you understand what I'm trying to say. So, I thought I would have more time to show my dad how much I cared for him, now all that is gone.

Looking back now as an adult with children I am thinking my upbringing was somewhat weird, but effective. Nevertheless, we survived, and we grew up without any repercussions, so something worked.

Not long after my father died, and as I tried every day to cope on a daily basis, I noticed my life in my home was changing as well, not for the better but for the worse. I noticed that my husband didn't seem like the person I married anymore. I began to notice great changes in him, which became very conspicuous to me. Because this was someone I knew since high school, I was able to pick up on any changes in his behavior, no matter imperceptible it may be. We dated for a few years before we got married, so obviously I was able to pick up on some things that were not customary.

"Most people do not clearly understand the word *abuse* . Visions of broken bones and black eyes are the generally held impressions. Certainly these severely physical indicators are signs of abuse, however, abuse can be much less noticeable and much more insidious" (Wilson, K. 2006, p. 8).

5

Some of these changes included making fun of my mistakes in the presence of his friends; not understanding how to use certain appliances such as the washing machine; taking a long time to understand the directions to various locations, among many others. All the simple things which would seem trivial to some, he would find them amusing at my expense. On many occasions I overheard him telling the individual (s) during his phone conversations how I couldn't grasp simple instructions. Sometimes I would join in and laugh just to sort of ease the pain I was feeling inside.

Nevertheless, in spite of the emotional and verbal abused endured, I ignored the changes for some time, thinking that they would eventually go away. This is one thing I learned growing up, ignoring a problem will not make it disappear, and instead it will become much worse. I realized now that that was the wrong thing to do.

> Abusive relationships are tricky and, just as a fish doesn't know that he's wet, we often don't see the subtle markers for abuse in a relationship because we are in it. Further, relationships fill our needs and, when our needs are being met, we don't necessarily have an imperative to take a look at how they are being met (Formica, M. 2014, par. 12).

So as a result of me not being familiar with my living location, and not knowing anyone in the area, I took up other interests in our home like reading, crafts among others. I had to do something in order to keep my sanity, because I was not able to contact or converse with my family back home in the islands. If I call them, or if they call me (collect), the charges would certainly be posted on the phone bill when it arrived; and not even Houdini would be able to make those bills and charges to disappear. Since I was not allowed to make or receive calls, I refrained from using the phone because it would certainly be an issue.

So rather than sitting around the house moping and feeling despondent, my son and I would do fun things together to pass the time away. We spent a lot of times playing games together, or reading. At times we would go into the backyard, and at the same time being careful not to establish any friendship with the neighbors next door, for fear that it would upset my husband.

Coming from a place where almost everything we do is done outdoors, you could tell what your neighbors are cooking as the aroma would rise up in the air and traveled into everyone's home. Everyone when your neighbors were home, when they were not home, where they went and when they returned home because every family had an open-door-policy. If my mom needed to borrow something from the neighbor (like salt, milk or sugar), she usually stand in front of our home and call out to the neighbor, and would receive a speedy comeback as the neighbor would respond with a shout.

So a sudden separation from that culture into this lifestyle where everyone stays behind not only closed, but locked doors, was really a stretch for myself as well as my son. It's not as if I visited this country before, in fact I never travelled outside of my country; so this was a whole new experience for me. It was especially difficult for my son too, because he was accustomed to running around to the neighbors' homes, and playing with the neighborhood children. This too was a new experience for him, and it took a long time for him to adjust.

Nevertheless, being grateful for the opportunity to come to the place where many never got the chance to visit, I decided to make the best of the situation on a daily basis.

CHAPTER 2

Hint, Hint!

Less than a year into my stay in this wonderful country I noticed more changes in my husband' behavior (not for the better), but I kept telling myself that his behavior was as a result of his stressful situations he experienced on the job, and maybe problems with co-workers. So I tried to be as understanding as I could, even if it meant me being uncomfortable. Drs. Sidney and Suzanne Simon say, "When betrayal occurs, we can almost hear a bond of trust snap and feel the pain rush in. We might feel as if we'd been slapped in the face" (Simon/ Simon, 1990, p.33). However in spite of me being understanding and empathetic, things got worse. I also started to notice and identify the 'little' things that caused him to get into his 'not so nice' mood. Things like:

- Not having dinner ready when he got home.
- If the dinner was ready, it wasn't hot enough, sometimes not cooked properly.
- As soon as he walked through the door, the dinner must be on its way to the dining table. Not before, not after.

- If our son is playing outside wearing sneakers only, and no socks.
- The meal was not served in the proper plates.
- The bed wasn't made properly.
- I wasn't wearing any lipstick.
- Constant complaint about the color of my lips being the same color as my skin, so I must wear make-up at all times.
- Constantly demanding respect without any thought about my needs.
- Forcing me to choose between him and my family, usually with the words "Remember who brought you here to this country" "Don't forget who saved you from a life of poverty"

  The list went on and on, in fact these are only a few of the many demands placed on me at the time.

After a while I felt like I was working as a housekeeper, with my husband as my employer with free room and board, only in my case I received no paycheck. It just did not seem like a marriage anymore because he addressed and corrected me as if I was a child, only the belt of correction was missing (well, actually not yet).

In my homeland, I watched my parents while I was growing up, how they did things together in harmony. I saw them weathered many storms together as they planted their crops and reaped together, and whatever one lacked, the other compensated. I always envisioned my marriage to be like theirs. So I tried to do everything possible in order to make sure that everything was right at home; I tried to put my personal feelings aside and try to make thing work. I thought that it was the duty and responsibility of a wife and mother to do whatever it takes to make her husband happy. Meg Dugan and Roger Hock say "Slowly you begin to realize that the troubling behavior was not going away; it was getting worse; it was becoming abusive. Still, even as the negative behavior increased, you might not have recognized it as abuse" (Dugan, Hock/2006, p. 10).

It is important to understand that everything I experienced was all new territory for me, so it was a day by day process. Before I embarked on this journey I was never counseled by my pastor or my parents. I was not given any tips on how to improve my marriage or how to deal with problems when they surface. I wasn't given those famous talks that many young women receive before they embark on such a journey. Getting married and relocating to another country happened so fast, and before I realized it I was thrust into the category of a wife and mother (back then at home my mother helped me greatly with my son). So the challenges were very overwhelming and many times very discouraging. There were several times when I imagined myself back home in my room curled up into bed reading a book, with not a care in the world. There were many times I was jolted back into reality and facing my responsibilities.

After a while I realized I was wearing myself down, nothing I did made any difference. Whatever I did was not good enough and the harder I tried to do things right, the more I made mistakes and ended up making a fool of myself. I gathered that I was falling apart because I was giving more than I had to give. Even though I am not a math genius, but even I understood that there was something wrong with that equation. I gradually realized that I did not have the power to keep things under control, it was too overpowering.

This is what happens when we try to do things without God, when we try to venture out on our own without Him, things have a way of backfiring on us. We try to cover up something very volatile with dirt and thinking that the dirt will keep it from exploding. It doesn't matter how deep the hole is dug, eventually the things covered will explode and destroy everything within its reach. As a result, situations will usually become much worse than before.

This is what happened in my marriage, I was living in a world where I tried so hard to convince myself that everything was okay, when in fact it wasn't. It wasn't very long before I saw my husband for the individual that he was. There was not a day that passed where I was not abused verbally in the presence of my children.

> Verbal abuse is warfare that employs the use of words as bombs and grenades designed to punish the other person, to place blame, or to justify one's own actions and decisions. Abusive language is filled with poisonous putdowns, which seek to make the other person feel bad, appear wrong, or look inadequate (Chapman, G., 2008, p. 122).

Wilson described some of the signs of verbal abuse as "Threatening to kill or use violence, accusing partner of unfaithfulness, making insinuations, yelling, using insults, being sarcastic, name-calling, sneering, criticizing, humiliating, laughing at partner, insulting family or friend (Wilson, K., 2006, p. 11-12)

CHAPTER 3

The Physical Abuse

A few years and another child later, I noticed that things got worse, because the focus was shifted from keeping the house a certain way, unto me. My baby was a few months old and I was still sporting my post-baby weight, so that bothered him. He was determined to get me back to the weight I was before, which was 112. I was forced to sit on his lap so he could tell if I went over the required weight limit. From my experience in life, if you really want to drag someone's self-esteem into the mud and trample on it, tell them how fat and ugly they are. Believe me: it can be very damaging. I tried so hard to keep my weight to the required number, even though it meant making myself miserable, in order to have a peaceful life. Mary Colson says "Every human being has a right to be respected and treated well. International laws and agreements protect human rights. An abuser is not respecting the rights of his or her victim" (Colson, 2011, p. 47).

He took the title 'head of household' to another level when he took it upon himself to buy the groceries (low fat this, low fat that; fat-free this, fat-free that, egg-white, lamb chops (Yuk) water, among other things). He did this without inquiring about

14

our preferences, although he knew that my son and I didn't like the things he liked. After a while, the idea of eating right and losing weight didn't seem exciting anymore. I began to remember my life back home when my sisters and I would be allowed to eat tasty meat dishes prepared by our mom, and our dad would give us preference in choosing our favorite parts of the animal, each time he slaughtered his animals to sell. I began to reminisce about my island patties, and our traditional bun and cheese eating days. I would give anything to be back home, because this fairy tale lifestyle didn't seem too enchanting to me anymore. Not only was I not allowed to shop for food, I also wasn't able or allowed to shop for clothes (undergarments included), because he purchased all the clothes for myself and the children. Of course he knew my clothes sizes, and they had better fit, or else... So I was what you would call a 'stay at home mom' because I literally 'stayed' at home.

I want to be clear about the issue of weight-loss. I am never against individuals losing weight because it is important for everyone to stay healthy. It protects one from sicknesses and diseases such as hypertension, diabetes, heart diseases among other problems. "It is a good idea to start healthy habits now. It will be easy for you to get used to healthy habits now and then you will have them for life" (Schaefer, A., 2010, p. 5).

However there is a big difference when one is being degraded and humiliated into losing weight. It defeats the purpose, and takes the fun out of exercising. It doesn't work, because the individual may lose the weight, but the process and effect can be very damaging. Although I managed to maintain that weight for quite some time, the exciting feeling that goes along with me losing weight was just not there. Instead, I felt miserable and unattractive. Of course my clothes fit nicely and I did receive compliments from friends, but feeling of satisfaction from losing the weight was lacking.

Very often I was ordered to stand on the scale to see if I exceeded my weight limit of 112 pounds. After a while I felt like I was weighed more often than the meat in the butcher store. If there was any slight weight gain, there would be problems such as verbal insults, of which I would always be on the receiving end.

Regardless, I suffered through the years, and thinking that it was alright, because I was certain that things would get better. In other words, the time-bomb was still covered, and was ticking. By now the tension in the home was so high that no one can climb over it. The spirit of malice, hatred and mischievousness moved in and became permanent residents in our home; well at least what was left of our home. When my husband became irritated about anything, he wouldn't speak to me for months, and if I decided to 'break the ice' by attempting to talk to him, he would respond with a few choice words, and I don't mean the good choice ones. Strangely enough I looked forward to those times when we didn't speak because it put a pause on the insults and gave me a break from that stupid scale. But when his anger subsided, and he decided to resume speaking to me again, here comes the measuring and the dieting again.

The effects of domestic violence or abuse can be very long and lasting. People who are abused by a spouse may experience an inability to sleep occasionally from recurring nightmares that produce a fear of being alone or being in certain physical surroundings. Depression or a constant feeling of dread may surround the daily life of an abused spouse. Many abused spouses experience anxiety attacks and cannot tolerate instant changes (Bishop, E-dee, 2009, p. 116).

It happened that the time came for my son to start school that left me with no one at home. So I became friends with my neighbor who lived a few houses away. One day she decided to visit me at home. For some reason I didn't get that memo which stated that I wasn't allowed to have anyone over, or visit anyone's home. So I thought 'Okay, another rule, I can live with that'.

On another day my friend called me on the phone. Another memo I didn't get, because he told my friend that I was not allowed to use the phone. I tried to remedy the situation by secretly going next door to use my other neighbor's phone to call my friend. I advised her to call my house and tell my husband that the call was a mistake because she called the wrong person. I guess I never read the book which teaches how to deceive the deceiver, because my husband somehow realized what I did and inquired from our neighbor if I used her phone. He discovered what I was trying to do, and became irritated. Of course I was 'punished' for trying to make a fool out of him (so he thought).

Now that I am looking back, I should've left things the way they were. I began to think 'so what if he cursed me, again? I should've been accustomed to his abuse by then. The thing was that, I tried so hard to make him happy at any cost, without even thinking of my wellbeing. And sometimes it backfired on me, which made things much worse, and caused him to label me as a liar when all I tried to do was to secure peace in the home. I was so focused on pleasing him that I ended making myself out to be someone I'm not.

This abuser was determined to have me to himself to physically and emotionally abuse me at his will, with no outside interference. His friends would look at me and the children and thought that we were the 'perfect' family, with well-mannered children and a wife who listened to her husband (little do they know that I had no choice). Many times I want to shout at these people because their compliments were making me sick. I wanted to yell out to them, to tell them what a deceiver their supposedly good friend was. I wanted to expose him for the monster that he was. Then I thought about what could possibly happen if I reveal his dark secrets, no-one would believe me anyway, so I played along with it.

So here I was in the home with someone who forgot his vows to love me 'for better or for worse', with no friends and suspended phone privileges (sounds like teenage punishment, right?). I was called all the names that are listed in and out of the dictionary (not the good ones, which would've been nice) and some he made up every so often.

If you have been defined by anyone, especially if by a parent or spouse, please begin this journey knowing that you are not what you've been told and you are not alone. Additionally, you do not deserve any negative behavior or attitude from the silent treatment to subtle implications, threats, name-calling, or any other abuse (Evans, P. 2012, p. 4).

When you've been degraded for years and called every possible vulgar name on a daily basis for years, it hurts. Imagine being reminded of these every day:

'You're no good'

'You are so stupid'

'You're so dumb'

'You cannot follow simple instructions'

'Did you go to school?'

'You can't make it without me'

'When I am through with you, no one will want you'

'You are going to regret the day you came to America' (In fact I was already regretting ever leaving my home sweet home).

'I own you'

'You will not amount to anything'

'I saved your life from poverty by bringing you here'

'If it wasn't for me, you and your family would have died from poverty'

'I made you who you are today'

Shouting is a form of verbal abuse. Verbal abuse can control, mock, embarrass, threaten and upset the victim. If someone shouts at you, it is shocking and can make you feel angry and upset. Constant yelling, threats and swearing are frightening. You may fear you will be physically harmed next. Don't put up with verbal abuse from abusers, tell them to stop and ask them to apologize (Colson, M., 20011 p.8).

Finally I resigned myself to the fact that all the things he said were true and I started to believe them, because I didn't think I would be anything else. Yes, I'm stupid, I can't do anything right and I will never become anyone worthwhile.

> An abuser can mistreat partner after partner in relationships, each time believing that the problems are the woman's fault and that he is the victim. Whether he presents himself as the victim of an ex-partner, or of his parents, the abuser's aim – though perhaps unconscious is to play on your compassion, so that he can avoid dealing with his problem (Bancroft, L., 2002, p. 29).

The verbal insults went on for a while, and it wasn't much longer after that, the physical abuse started. It was as if I knew that any day it would happen because of the way the arguments were escalating and intensifying. It was only a matter of time before he started to show me what he actually was made of (his true character). Once the physical abuse started, things went from bad to worse. To be very honest with you, I couldn't tell you which hurt more, the physical abuse or the verbal abuse. Whoever wrote the slogan "sticks and stones may break my bones, but words can't", they lied to us. Believe me, they both hurt, equally.

Dr. Kathy Crisp says

> Whatever I do in the relationship is never good enough. I've experienced both physical and emotional abuse, and I'd much rather be beaten. I have no self-worth at this

point. I keep trying to pull myself back up, but I'm not getting anywhere. My abuser has helped me stay stuck. I never want to get out of bed, and that's not me. That's not who I believe I really am. It's definitely not who I want to be. I feel as though I'm being suffocated (Crisp, 2010, p. 57).

He had no remorse for the way he treated me, and no intention of apologizing for the verbal abuse he inflicted in me over the years. He felt that whatever he did was for my own good, because I needed to be 'straightened out' or 'taught a lesson'. Whenever he would hit me, he blamed me for making him angry, it was always my fault. Why on earth would I do anything wrong intentionally just so he could abuse me?

> The verbal abuser, on the other hand, seldom asks for forgiveness or acknowledges that the verbal tirades are inappropriate. Typically, the abuser will blame the spouse for stimulating the abuse. "She got what she deserved" is the attitude of the abuser (Chapman, G., 2008, p. 122).

Looking back over the years, I've often wondered how I caused someone to abuse me. How did I allow myself to be beaten and scarred by another and not being able to prevent it from happening? When and how did it started? It all happened in such a deceitful way that before I realized I was receiving my daily dose of beatings on a constant basis.

I was constantly told that I asked for it so I got what I deserved. I didn't remember submitting any requests to be abused. It appeared that whatever I did or said, it was a request to be hit or yelled at. At times I was afraid to even move, or say anything, just in case he misinterpreted my actions as a request for a 'beating'

During my marriage I received so many black eyes and bruised arms, necks, backs and shoulders that one would think that I was constantly on the losing end of a boxing match. I slowly began to look like a bruised fruit with black and blue marks all over my body. I got so tired of telling people that I fell down the stairs, or I walked into a wall. People were probably thinking "Is she blind? She's always walking into walls and falling down stairs?" I became such a good liar that I even began to convince myself that I did in fact walked into those walls and fell down the stairs. A lie detector couldn't prove otherwise. Richard Davis says "Although it is most often hidden from public view, violence in our homes is a problem that we all should be universally conscious of. Yet many of us, both men and women, often deny its existence" (Davis, 1998, p.2).

So as a result, a beautiful, bright young lady with a good heart, with plans to further her studies as a nurse, who had so much to offer, was gradually transformed into someone of very little worth, with very low self-esteem, whose life was at a standstill. I began to believe that I was nothing, will be nothing and will never be anyone worthwhile. "I was that low. I felt like nothing. I couldn't even hold my head up on the street. I just felt like ... I just felt like nothing, and then having someone telling you constantly you're nothing" (Abrahams, H., 2010, p. 21).

CHAPTER 4

Taking It to the Streets

One cold afternoon (while I was still pregnant with our second child) we were traveling to another city when an argument started (this is usually a one-man participation where only he argued). He didn't care that our son was sitting in the back seat of the car, so he started his ranting and raving. It was strange to see someone so irritated if the wind blew too hard across his face, or if another driver cuts him off on the road. He was a very, very angry young man and that was scary.

I was eight months pregnant, feeling very irritable, with hormones who had minds of their own, I wasn't in the mood for his ranting on that day. I guessed that was a day when my cup became full and was running over, so I did the unthinking, the unimaginable. I responded! Yes, I sure did. I realized that I was treading on dangerous ground, but I was frustrated and at the point where I didn't care. Then there was this little man sitting on my shoulder daring to me to 'speak, speak, speak'. So I did. There was silence in the car. Then he asked "what did you say?" I repeated 'leave me alone'. It felt good, and seeing his silence I thought to myself "I'm going to start speaking up for myself from now on" "I now have a voice", "good for me, yeah". He appeared to be angry due to the fact that for the first time in years, this silent partner of his, finally had a voice.

He was quiet for a while and I was sitting there thinking that I did something good for once. I thought that everything was okay, until we came to the first shopping mall, he drove into a parking space and demanded me to get out of the car, I did not respond nor did I move, so he got out of the car, came to my door, opened it and ordered me out of the car. I refused to get out because it was cold and moreover I wasn't back home where I could easily walk back to my house. I did not even know what part of town I was, so I stood (in this case, sat) my ground, refusing to leave. Without a second thought, he reached for my hand, dragged me out of the car, threw me on the ground, hopped back in the driver's seat and drove away. I sat there on the ground dazed, because everything happened so fast. My body felt numb, probably because of the weather, or maybe I was still in shock.

> Perpetrators of domestic violence variously beat, kick, strangle, stab, rape and shoot their wives. Women are locked in their homes to isolate them from their natal families and to prevent them from seeking assistance; are denied food; and are beaten with bricks, pipes and other heavy objects. They are humiliated and demeaned. Some women are hospitalized due to domestic abuse, some suffer permanent injury. Women are severely traumatized by the violence they experienced and some commit suicide as a result. Some are killed by their husband (Shields, A., p. 1, 2006).

After some time I managed to get myself off the ground, not knowing where I was and didn't even remember my address in case someone should ask. The thought never occurred to me to call the police, because for me it was an embarrassing situation. Moreover I had no money to call anyone (there were no cell-phones then). I stood there in the parking lot crying and fearing the worst. Considering the time of the year this incident happened, I was also freezing. Eve and Carl Buzawa say "Many assailants immaturely externalize blame for violence to the victim with comment such as 'she provoked me' thereby rationalizing otherwise inexcusable conduct" (Buzawa/Buzawa, 2003, p. 36).

Several hours later when it got pretty dark, he returned and picked me up. The ride home was very quiet as neither of us spoke; instead he acted as if nothing happened. I wanted to say what was on my mind, I wanted to hit him, and I also thought of a few choice words (trust me, they were bad). But considering what happened that morning I learned my lesson, which was to keep my mouth shut.

Men express many feelings through violence and their feelings may determine their actions. Men may enjoy inflicting violence. 'The, more violence he did to me, the happier he would be.' 'After he had hit me, he would say 'Sit here in front of me, if I see any tears in your eyes then see what happens.' Then he would say 'Laugh and talk with me.' (Hanmer, J., Itzin, C., 2000, p. 12).

My husband did not apologize, no mention of the day's events, nothing. At that point I didn't really care, all I wanted was a warm shower, something to eat and warm clothes. Gary Thomas says "I believe that one of marriages' primary purposes is to teach us how to forgive" (Thomas, 2000, p. 167). Looking back to the happenings of that day and other days, I am convinced that his problem was more than just anger. At times he would become angry at me for reasons I didn't understand, then he would hit me. It was as if he would make himself angry on purpose just so he could find a reason to hit me. After each attack, he would stand there and stare at me as if in a daze. It was as if he was not aware of his actions.

I recalled a time when things were going quite well for us, we were being civil towards each other and there were very few disagreements. This went on for several weeks and I began to think that things were getting back to the way they were. I was happy, he was happy and so were the children. It happened that one morning I was being affectionate to my husband, only to be roughly pushed away. Surprisingly I inquired what happened, after all it was quite early in the morning. To my astonishment, he told me that he was mad at me because I was being disrespectful to him in his dreams. I stood there speechless for quite some time because I couldn't believe what he said. I could not respond because frankly I was at a loss for words.

It was then I realized that his actions were those of a disturbed individual who needed help. It was as if he was a ticking time bomb, waiting to explode. It was also a sign for me to get out, and get out fast.

> A common phrase expressed by a family member when describing an episode of rage is 'going off.' This means a tirade takes place with ranting and raving over some issue. Very little, if any communication or problem solving takes place during an episode of rage. Excessive agitation and anger are clearly released, however, the anger is projected in a damaging way onto family members. The abuser finds fault and externalizes blame while in a tirade with others (Woulas, M., 2010, p. 62).

From that day I didn't make the effort to salvage our relationship, in fact I began to enjoy the silent treatment, because I didn't think there was any chance of a better life with us.

The spirit of boldness penetrated my body one night as we were returning home from a family get-together. He was on the war-path; apparently I didn't present myself worthy to be his wife. He complained that I did not smile enough or I wasn't talkative enough. I made certain to sit in the back seat because I was tired and wanted to go home, and not in the mood for his ranting and raving that night. He was the life of the party, there were no sign that he was displeased about anything. Yet as soon as we were in the car his demeanor changed. As he started to drive. I noticed that he was up to something because his emotions suddenly changed. He cursed me shamefully and I sat in the back seat of the car in tears. He was driving on the highway real fast and the insults were spewing out of his mouth.

It was one of those times when I was tired and wasn't about to put up with his insults, so I positioned myself in a way where he couldn't reach me, and I hit him in the back of his head. You can imagine how shocked he was, because ever since the time he pulled pregnant me out of the car, I kept my words to myself. Seeing that he was driving he couldn't retaliate the way he wanted to, so he started with more verbal abuse. Each time he called me names, I would hit him. Then he tried to hit me while one of his hands was on the steering wheel, but seeing that I was only 112 pounds he couldn't reach me (at that time my skinny size paid off). I was sitting in the seat directly behind him so each time he swung at me, he missed. His words hurt so bad that I thought I wasn't hitting him hard enough, so I grabbed his shirt with such force that a piece of it came off into my hand. As he cursed me, I ripped his shirt, all the way until we got home. By the time we got into the driveway, he was only sporting his tie, and a small piece of his shirt in his hand, which he managed to salvage. I knew then that my life was over, but I didn't care because I was tired of the insults. At least I could say that I went down fighting because I was fed up.

My husband, in his clever ways didn't say anything as he walked up the driveway and opened the door. I thought about not going into the house, but then where would I go? I waited for him to go inside then I reluctantly went inside. I hurried up the stairs and went into the guest room, locked the door and went to bed.

The next day his friends came to the house and the interrogation started. According to them, I was the worse person in the world for attacking my husband in such vicious way. There was no room for my defense, because they were already convinced that I was the aggressor in the relationship. They reminded me of how 'lucky' I was to have such a caring, loving and dedicated husband. They also told me that he could've had any woman he wanted, but he chose to return home to the islands and brought me here. By the end of the week, everyone (including family members and friends) heard about the horrible thing I did. The only time I lifted a hand to defend myself, I was labeled as the worse person in the world. At that time it seemed like a battle I could never win, because all odds were against me.

> The strongest risk factor for being a victim of domestic violence is being a woman. According to the U.S. Department of Justice, there were 691,710 reported acts of non-fatal violence committed by current or former spouses, boyfriends or girlfriends in 2001. In 85 percent of these assaults the crimes were committed by men against women. A Commonwealth Fund Survey reports that nearly one third (3) percent of American women report being physically or sexually abused by an intimate partner at some point in their lives. (Wilson, K., 2006, p. 8)

CHAPTER 5

And More Abuse

At this point in the relationship, I felt the need to get away. I felt that if I didn't get away as fast and as far as I could, I would not last very long. "Women are at a greater risk of violence from their partners when they attempt to leave and for several months after" (Howard, L., Feder, G., Agnew-Davies, R., 2013, p. 12). After my child was born, I was excited but somewhat sad, because I was forced back into getting weighed again and eating diet food. During my pregnancy I must admit that I enjoyed 'eating for two' because it was to my liking. I enjoyed my pregnancy because I gave birth to another handsome baby boy, but I enjoyed the nine months where I wasn't being ridiculed because of the way I looked, because of my weight, or the types of foods I ate.

So, after my son's birth (by C-section) I was handed sweat suits and other exercise gear because according to him, I had to return to weighing 112 pounds (I began to hate those numbers). So my 'free' days were over and I was back to my exercise routine. I lost the weight very quickly and according to outsiders I looked great, but inside I was hurting so bad. I learned from this experience that one cannot be judged solely from what is seen on the outside.

I looked okay outwardly but on the inside I was such a messed-up individual. People will often see the outside of an individual and believed that everything is alright without getting to know more about the person. This experience has taught me the importance of not judging others. It is definitely hard to tell from the outside looking in, that everything is alright.

One day as I was driving, I remembered praying to God (I haven't prayed in so many years), yet I decided to inquire from God what have I done for Him to allow so many bad things to happen to me. I started out with many questions, like Job:

"Lord why do you hate me?"

"You took me from my family with in my hometown to die here in misery?"

'You say you care about people, is this how you show it?"

I remembered arguing "I've never killed anyone, and you allowed me to be treated like this"

"What kind of a loving God are you?"

Like Job I waited for answers, and I wanted my answers not in years to come, but at that minute, I wanted answers to my questions at that time. I felt Job's pain when he said

> And now my soul is poured out upon me; the days of affliction have taken hold upon me. My bones are pierced in me in the night season: and my sinews take no rest. By the great force of my disease is my garment changed: it bindeth me about as the collar of my coat. He hath cast me into the mire, and I am become like dust and ashes (Job 30:16-19, KJV).

Like Job I wondered, I questioned, I inquired but no response; then when there was nothing else in my power to do, I waited. So I thought to myself that maybe God doesn't care about people the way it's written in the Bible. So the thought came to me to just end it all for my boys and myself, because I didn't see any way out of this. I couldn't use the phone to call my family back in my hometown, I had no friends, I lost my self-respect, my dignity. I was regarded as the abuser in my marriage by everyone we knew, so what's the use? I felt like dirt.

> How we respond to any given psychological stress is entirely up to us, which by itself is a huge problem. It takes an enormous degree of character to choose to be responsible for all that occurs in your life and to realize that even you can't control all of the events, you can control how you feel about it (Weinstein, R., 2004, n.p).

One day I picked up my children from the babysitter, and as I was driving I had the idea to drive the car off the road with my boys and end our lives of misery. Then there would be no more hurt, no more insults or beatings. At least my husband would have no one else to beat upon. The fact that he wanted to be in control always, he would probably just go and find someone else to abuse. As a result I thought of doing that unpardonable deed, I glanced at my boys in the back-seat (while at the stop sign of course), and there they were sitting in the back seat fighting with each other. Immediately I smiled and kept driving, but this time with a renewed desire to survive. "Hurting yourself is not the answer. It is natural to feel down and angry when you are hurt, and you may think suicide is the only way out. It isn't. Use that anger instead to fuel the energy needed to take care of yourself" (Cobb, C., 2001, p. 80). Lynn Shipway also say "The violence becomes insidious, permeating every action, every thought and deed until eventually, for some women, suicide remains the only escape" (Shipway/ 2004, p. 1).

Looking back then I realized that even though I thought that God had forgotten and abandoned me, it was in fact the opposite, because He was in right there holding my hand and guiding me through. I believe that on that day Satan hopped into the car and tried to convince me that my life was hopeless, and that I should end it all. But God stepped in and said "NO! You can't have them". God saw me ranting and raving on many occasions, accusing Him of everything that happened to me in my life. And during those times, He never left my side. Even though I thought that He had forsaken me, He was in fact nearby just in case I needed Him.

Since then I felt better and stronger, I felt a renewed sense of survival; even though on many occasions I cried myself to sleep at nights as the abuse continued. I remembered many nights I cried so much that I became very sick. Then I would wake up in the mornings with excruciating headaches which sometimes lasted throughout the day.

When there is no one to encourage you and to help you to get through the rough days, and nights it becomes more difficult and unbearable. I am thankful to my Heavenly Father that the many times when I wasn't thinking about Him, He was thinking about me. Today He is still doing the same thing for me and for you also. It may appear that you are facing your trials alone, but He's always close by just in case we need Him.

CHAPTER 6

From Worse to Worst

My life as a wife battling domestic abuse continued for much longer as the years passed by. This involved the beatings, the emotional, verbal and psychological mistreatment.

"Physical abuse is often the most easily recognized form of abuse. Physical abuse can be any kind of hitting, shaking, burning, pinching, biting, choking, throwing, beating, and other actions that cause physical injury, leave marks, or cause pain" (DuPont, A., 2014, par. 4).

It happened that I woke up one morning and started to comb my hair, and to my surprise my long, flowing hair began to leave my scalp at each combing. Before I realized it, I was going bald, which wasn't helpful to my self-esteem (no offence to those who are experiencing baldness as they battle various illnesses). I thought I lost everything there was to lose, then losing my hair was added to the list. Then I realized that whatever was going on my inside, was eventually showing on the outside.

I was at the point in my life where I had to run, and fast. So I resumed my plans to find a way to escape, with the understanding that the process would not be easy. I was threatened numerous times that wherever I decided to go, I would be found, and probably harmed or killed. So I started to think of ways to escape even if I had to return home to the islands as a bald and skinny woman.

It happened that one night while my husband was away for the weekend, the boys and I were watching a movie in the living room. As we were laughing and having fun, Mr. Scrooge came home, walked into the living room and turned off the television. Then he started his abusive routine, so I sent the boys upstairs to their room. I sat there listening to him cursing and being abusive. Sometime ago he would need reasons to rant, but he became so accustomed to that way of life that he didn't need a reason to be abusive. I guess that finally it became a part of him. He was so full of anger, which was unexplainable.

> Anger seems to have two purposes: first, anger is our emotional SOS. It is a loud message clearly stating that there is a problem. It is a psychological flare gun that informs those nearby that something is wrong, out of balance or unjust. Anger as a defense declares that something needs to be straightened, fixed or even destroyed (Sells, J., Yarhouse, M., 2011, p. 99).

He was out of town for the weekend, why would he come home to abuse me? What did I do? So I waited for him to 'come up for air' then out of frustration, that little man hopped on my shoulder again and dared me to speak. So I responded "Fine, I'll just take my kids and leave". For a moment I felt like I was in the twilight zone. It was the same way I felt before he dragged me out of the car (it was not so long ago but I forgot the experience) then the same feeling returned, that awkward, eerie silence. I knew something was coming, and it was coming my way.

I turned around and felt someone hit me on the right side of my face. I glanced at my white dress and it instantaneously turned red as a result of the blood from my face. I thought I lost a part of my face because the blood was gushing from my face. My immediate reaction was to scream real loudly out of fear, but the kids heard my screams and came racing downstairs only to be chased back up the stairs by their dad. If I decided to alert the police, I wouldn't be able to say what happened because everything happened so fast. I stood there in the living room for a while, scared and trying to figure out what happened to me. Up to that time I did not know the extent of my injuries because I was covered in blood. I was even afraid to remove the blood from my face because I thought half of my face was gone. He stood there staring at me as if he was seeing a ghost, then he went upstairs to his bed I wanted to go to the hospital that night, but I thought that if I alert the authorities and he was arrested, I wouldn't have anywhere to stay. The thoughts came racing through my mind and I became even more confused. Feeling alone and with the terrible pain I was experiencing, I decided to lay down. I spent the night in the couch, and for the next couple of weeks I could not go outside because my face was so swollen, and I was sporting a huge cut on my face. The attack on me that night has been a constant reminder today because my face is permanently scarred.

This individual tried so hard to prove to me that he was the boss, which I had no problem as long as it is done the right way. An individual does not have to beat upon another just to prove that he or she is in charge. I perceived that person to be nothing more than a coward who try to dominate another person, especially those he or she promised to love and cherish. Gary Chapman says "Dominant personalities are goal-oriented. They get things done, but they often hurt people in the process" (Chapman, 2008, p. 90).

After all that happened, I started to have heart-to-heart talks to myself. I became more convinced from then on that if I stayed, I would not make it to my next birthday.

From then, the physical abuse became a daily ritual, there was always something I did to make him angry enough to hit me. I remembered one day he hit me so hard with the broom, and I raised my hand to block the hit, but the broom hit my hand instead. For a week I was unable to remove my wedding ring from my finger because my hand was so swollen.

On another occasion, he was angry because my friend rang our door bell to speak to me. Not realizing that he heard the doorbell also, I quietly slipped outside and closed the door behind me. I tried to hurry the conversation for fearing that she would recognize that I was being abused. I managed to chat with her for a few minutes then I hurriedly say goodbye and sneaked back into the house. To my surprise he was standing behind the door eavesdropping on our dialogue, and as soon as I locked the door behind me, he grabbed me. This was another time I appreciated being skinny because I was able to slipped away from him and ran upstairs. He followed me into the bathroom and hit me with such force that I fell backwards in the bathtub, hitting the back of my head. I was unable to move for quite some time because I was in a daze for a very long time. Adding the incidents mentioned to the many that were omitted, are more than enough reasons for me to get out while I was still breathing.

CHAPTER 7

A Light, At Last

It happened that one day one of his friends decided to stop by and he noticed that something wasn't right with me. I became very withdrawn and I avoided anyone who came to visit. After asking me several questions, I decided to confide in him. So from then on he kept in constant communication with me. It was such a relief to finally found someone who would listen to me. After several months passed, my friend and his wife revealed to me that his job required him to relocate to another part of the country. He then suggested that I relocate with him and his family and start my life over. That sounded great, but how? It sounded good but seemed impossible. So, with no money, no connections, I immediately dismissed the idea.

The end of the year came and I understood from my husband's phone calls that he was making plans to spend the Christmas holidays in another country (without the kids and me of course). There goes that little light in my head again. I thought that the time was so perfect, but being programmed as a submissive wife for so long, I didn't think I had what it took to make a clean getaway. Moreover he could easily locate me and then I would be dead for sure. So, again I dismissed the thought.

The next day I gave my friend my response and as was expected, he became angry and reminded me of the numerous times that I was abused. So I gathered a bit of courage and finally said yes.

For the next several weeks before his vacation, I endured more insults and more beatings, but because I knew my plans, the abuse became bearable. Finally the day came when he packed and left for his vacation. The next morning still nervous I called the movers to have my things packed away in storage. My friend paid for my boys and me to stay in a hotel, which was another step in my plans to escape. Even though things were going well, I was very nervous and scared.

Then there was a setback which caused me to start writing my obituary: my friend's plans to relocate were now delayed, which meant that our stay in the hotel would be extended. That meant my husband would return from his vacation before we leave for our new location. Then my fears started to roll back and I began to panic. I had every reason to panic because sure enough, just as I thought, my husband returned and obviously he discovered that we moved out.

A few days later I heard that he was searching for us. If ever I experienced having a nervous breakdown before, that was it. I remained locked up inside that hotel unable to sleep or eat. My poor heart was beating so fast, I felt it wanted to leave my distressed body. For every day for another week I couldn't sleep because I began to think that I made a big mistake.

Until one afternoon, I heard someone pounding heavily on the door, and I knew who it was, so the children and I rushed to hide in the bathtub. After sometime, I decided to call the authorities, who advised me not to open the door. I later realized that they were not coming to my rescue, so I fearfully opened the door. I figured that the longer he banged on the door, the angrier he would become. As I opened the door, I thought to myself, 'well, this is it'. Whatever happened, I was prepared to deal with it. If he killed me out of anger, well! So be it.

To my surprise, he walked in and held on to me, I tried to escape his grasp but he held on to me, begging me to return with the boys. I stood there staring at him, half scared and half bold, half something, but not showing my emotions. He realized that I wasn't responding to him, so he fell on his knees and cried, and being the soft-hearted person that I am, I too cried. All the years we've been dating from high school until now, I never saw him cried, never begged, never apologized, and never kneeled. I felt so sorry for him because he seemed so calm. I thought to myself that maybe has changed.

Jalna Hanmer and Catherine Itzin say "After violent attacks or when women leave, men frequently utilize several strategies simultaneously in response. These include tears, apologies and expressions of a desire for the relationship to continue, 'When I left he comes down and says 'I'm really sorry, please come back.' He would cry."

So I said to myself 'I am returning home because my husband needed me and the boys". I promised to return to the home within a few weeks, he even promised to help me return my belongings to the home as soon as I was ready to return. For the next couple of days I walked around like a mechanical person with no mind of my own. I felt like I had strings being pulled in every direction, and not knowing what to do. Strangely enough, I still loved my husband and for the first in a very long time, I felt like he loved me too. Then I thought about the beatings, the black-eyes, and the scars on my face, my bruised and battered body. Then I recalled that he apologized and begged me to return, which never happened before. Talking about a confused individual, I was that person. Dr. Les Parrot says:

> Unfortunately, you are up against a full-throttle, no-holds-barred bundle of regrets that are weighing you down in countless ways. You are plagued by if-onlys. Your past is dictating your future. Your regrets have lingered far too long and have evolved into guilt over not only what you have done but who you have become. Your shroud of shame envelopes your personality, and it is time to break free from the cocoon you have made of your emotions (Parrott/2003, p. 22).

So the next week I called up my friend to tell him of my change of plans. He rushed over to the hotel and he shook all 112 pounds of me (in a nice way), and asked if I was crazy. He began to remind me of the things I experienced at the hands of this abusive person, the black eyes, busted lips, and bruised marks all over my body. He also reminded me that apart from him, I had no real friends in that part of town, and when he leaves and the abuse started again, he won't be around to rescue me. His words hit home when he told me that the next time I may not survive. Well I must say that my friend's firm words did a good job convincing me because the next thing I knew the two boys and myself were on a plane destined for another state.

CHAPTER 8

Freedom

My first night in my new location, I slept like a baby, in fact much better than a baby. I woke up the next morning feeling so great that my body aches and pains did not even matter. My friend and his family lived quite a distance from where my boys and I were staying. I wasn't concerned about the fact that I was in new place so far away from them, so long as I was a good distance away from my tormentor. I felt as if I dropped 50 pounds of stress, I did not realize how heavy a load I was carrying for all those years. Dr. Archibald Hart says "In dedication to hindering the body's defense systems, stress can also lead to illness by disrupting normal functions more directly and damaging the tissue of the body" (Hart., 1995, n.p). Dr. Joseph Goldberg also adds "Stress that continues without relief can lead to a condition called distress -- a negative stress reaction. Distress can lead to physical symptoms including headaches, upset stomach, elevated blood pressure, chest pain, and problems sleeping. Research suggests that stress also can bring on or worsen certain symptoms or diseases." (Goldberg, 2014, par. 4). Harne also says

In Humphrey and Thiara's study of 180 women who had used Women's Aid Outreach Services, 60 percent had left as a result of being threatened with being killed (Humphreys and Thiara, 2003). On separation the women in this study who had experienced life-threatening violence or threats of being killed continued to experience extreme fear, which could involve flashbacks, panic attacks and sleeplessness (sometimes defined in medical discourse as post-traumatic stress disorder) as is indicated by one survivor's account from this study (Harne, L., 2008, p. 42).

I realized that having the boys made it difficult for me to get around, so I decided to return to my homeland where they could stay with my mom for a while. Throughout my ordeal, my main focus was on surviving each day, there was no thought about my appearance; I even forgot that I lost most of my hair. I realized how bad I looked when I arrived home and my mom looked at me and cried, especially when she saw my hair (at least what was left of it). She cried even more when I told her of the things I endured. Being the loving mother that she is, she braided my hair every day, and when it was time for me to return, I had hair again. Not only that, I gained weight, no longer 112 pounds (when it comes to gaining weight, the island food will do it all the time). As a result I started to plan my life again.

Upon returning, I was able to complete the nursing program I started initially, and was subsequently employed by a nursing agency. I was able to save enough money to allow my mom to escort the boys back to me. Seeing that I wasted so many years of my life in torment I decided to embrace each day with thankfulness, because I realized how close I came to losing my life. I had a whole new outlook on life and I began to look forward to my new life of raising my children in the proper way.

Months passed before I received word that my husband was looking for me. According to him, he knew where I was and he was coming to get me, and I would regret the day I was born. "Sometimes leaving an abusive situation and restoring your self-esteem is not enough to free yourself. Stalking is another form of abuse a person may resort to after a breakup" (Cobb, C., 2001, p. 80).

I remembered watching those mafia movies, and if someone says he's coming to get you, it's not going to be a happy reunion, I knew it was bad. All the old, painful feelings came rushing back, so I started to panic again, I had an Elijah moment and decided to run and hide. 1 Kings 19:1-3 says

> And Ahab told Jezebel all that Elijah had done, and withal how he had slain all the prophets with the sword. Then Jezebel sent a messenger unto Elijah, saying, So let the gods do to me, and more also, if I make not thy life as the life of one of them by tomorrow about this time. And when he saw that, he arose, and went for his life, and came to Beersheba, which belongeth to Judah, and left his servant there (KJV).

I informed my friend of the threatening messages, and he made the long trip from where he resided to 'straighten' me out again. He assured me that there was no way my husband could locate me, and I if he did, I didn't have to return with him. I knew he was correct, but I was so brainwashed by my abuser over the years that if he said he could find me, I believed he could. In my mind, nothing was impossible for him, everything he said he would do, I was convinced that he could make it happen. I believed that he was that powerful.

In spite of everything I returned to work, but each time I walked down the street I always looked over my shoulders, so to speak. Because I was afraid that he would find me and probably harm me for leaving him, and for taking the boys with me. Standing at the bus stops each day, I always felt as if someone was behind me, nevertheless I managed to get on with my life. Leaving my abusive lifestyle was not working out as well as I thought because I began to have mixed feelings. I was at a point where I didn't know what was good for me anymore. People thought I was crazy to leave my stable home and not knowing where I was going or what I was doing. No one actually thought about how unhappy I was.

> I was to blame for his abuse and I couldn't manage to figure how to be the sort of wife he cherished which he promised he surely would – if I could just learn how to make him happy. A wife who can't make her husband happy; why would I want that to become public knowledge? I agreed to the character that I played my part well which probably explains why. When I finally did leave, he got to keep the friends; no one understood why I'd want to leave such a charming man. (Weiss, E., 2004, p. 24).

Each day I became more confused about my move, some good and some bad. I sometimes became fearful wondering if I could make it in life as a single mother. Being raised at home with my sisters with no traveling experience only to be thrust into a life as a wife and mother, was not easy. Then years after, and two kids later I was thrust into another stage of my life which I had no knowledge of. It was hard trying to raise them as a single parent. My mother being here with me helped tremendously as she cared for the boys while I worked at different nursing agencies. Yet even though the childcare aspect was covered, it was as if something was still missing from my life. It was very, very difficult for me, especially since I was not yet a believer. So focusing on the responsibilities I had to face, some days seemed bearable, while some days appeared downright impossible and overwhelming. The overwhelming days far outweighed the bearable ones, yet I was determined to persevere. Many nights I went to bed feeling more confused than ever. I would cry myself to sleep many nights, and at the same time being careful that my mom and my sons could not hear me.

Your strengths and weaknesses are part of your everyday life. Reinforce your strengths and eliminate your weaknesses. You can reinforce your strength easily by doing mirror exercises. Look in the mirror when you wake up and before you go to bed every night. Become your own best friend. Say positive things to yourself. This may sound corny, but your brain will pay attention (Bettino, C., 2009, p.47).

CHAPTER 9

Life After Domestic Abuse

I don't know if it is possible that an abused person can actually overcome domestic abuse, for me it is and still is a gradual, day by day process. Even today, over twenty years later whenever I hear stories of others who were abused, it appeared that I am reliving the experiences all over again. It was a very heavy burden which I carried for many years, and did not even realize the frustrations it caused.

On that unforgettable day when I became a child of God, I gladly gave Him all my burdens just as the scripture requested. 1 Peter 5:7 says "Casting all your care upon him; for he careth for you." (KJV). That is why after so many years of silence, I am able to share my stories so others can share theirs too. My prayer is that as a result of my testimony, many will be helped as they read my story. After I relocated, it was quite some time before I started attending church because I was more focused on raising my children. I thought to myself that they were more important than anything or anyone, so I dedicated myself to parenting.

I tried very hard to stay busy because periodically I remembered my unpleasant, abusive experience, and each time

I remembered, it made me sad, and sometimes angry. I also remembered how close I came to losing my sanity and probably my life, I sometimes go into a room and cried. Then there were other times I wondered if I did the right thing by leaving. I even wondered how I would ever make it on my own, seeing that I was never so far away from home before. There were so many mixed emotions that I even became confused at times and often wondered if I should return to my husband's place. I worry most about me failing to survive on my own, and how my husband would be happy to know that I failed to make it without him. I began to think 'what if all those things he said about me were true?', 'what if I was no good, just as he said?' It was as if I was being miserable all over again. It wasn't easy shaking those negative, derogatory things that were spoken over you all those years.

Starting on a different pathway in our lives is always exciting and a little frightening. Whether it is a comparatively small step, such as signing up to learn a new skill or a major change – starting a new job, moving to a new home, or even a new country – we have expectations about what it will be like, hopes about how we would like things to turn out and speculation as to what it might lead to. But there will also be fears about what lies ahead and whether we will be able to make a success of it. Some of these feelings may be shaped by past memories of success or failure, either by the positive or negative attitudes of those around us by what we have read or people we meet who have done the same thing. (Abrahams, H., 2010, 0. 17).

CHAPTER 10

It's in the Church

As I continued my research I realized that domestic abuse does not only happens in the secular world, but shockingly in the Christians' homes and churches as well. Domestic abuse certainly does not discriminate, which is why it is so important to tackle it before it tackles us. Christians abusing each other whether in this fashion or in other ways, is another route used by the enemy in his attempt to hinder the progression of God's work. It is important for the church to help it members who are silently suffering from this form of abuse.

Amid growing world recognition of the problems women face, everyday fears, the bruises and battering they experience, and the needs of their children for safety and security, where are the churches? Why have religious groups been so slow to respond to victims' cries for help? Indeed, amid ever-increasing number of men and women world-wide who recognize the severity of woman abuse and have personal and professional commitment to work towards its elimination. Where are God's people, called in God's name to bring healing in the midst of suffering? (Anderson, Jocelyn, 2007, p. 15).

It is evident from the Bible stories, that physical and domestic abuse can be dated back to Bible times. This tells me that the devil is dedicated to his cause of destroying God's people. Therefore it is important for us to make every effort to transfer our knowledge to each other so that we'll be more impervious to his tricks and lies. It is important for us to write our stories so that others will not only hear about them, but will also know how we overcame. I love the Lord's instructions to Moses in Exodus 17:14 says "And the LORD said unto Moses, Write this for a memorial in a book, and rehearse it in the ears of Joshua" (KJV). There are several Bible stories that provide evidence of abuse.

- In the book of Genesis, Cain became jealous of his brother Abel, and killed him. According to chapter 4:8-9 "And Cain talked with Abel his brother: and it came to pass, when they were in the field, that Cain rose up against Abel his brother, and slew him. And the LORD said unto Cain, Where is Abel thy brother? And he said, I know not: Am I my brother's keeper?" (KJV).
- Abigail was a strong Christian woman who lived in an abusive relationship for quite some time. Her husband, whose name was Nabal, despite his great wealth, was very obnoxious and discourteous both to his wife and others.1 Samuel 25:3 say "Now the name of the man was Nabal; and the name of his wife Abigail: and she was a woman of

good understanding, and of a beautiful countenance: but the man was churlish and evil in his doings; and he was of the house of Caleb" (KJV).

- The Biblical story of Saul and David help us to understand the unusual relationship between them. The scripture says that Saul made several attempts on David's life because of jealousy. Another way that Saul showed signs of domestic abuse was when he tried to sever the relationship between his son Jonathan and David. 1 Samuel 19:9-10 says "But an evil[a] spirit from the LORD came on Saul as he was sitting in his house with his spear in his hand. While David was playing the lyre, [10] Saul tried to pin him to the wall with his spear, but David eluded him as Saul drove the spear into the wall. That night David made good his escape (KJV).

- Saul also tried to hinder David from returning to his home. Abusers, whether male or female have a tendency to separate his or her victims from those who may be able to render assistance to the one who is being abused. According to Lundy Bancroft

The unifying principle is his attitude of ownership. The batterer believes that once you are in a committed relationship with him, you belong to him. This possessiveness in batterers is the reason why killing of battered women so commonly happen when victims are attempting to leave the relationship; a batterer does not believe that his partner has the right to end a relationship until he is ready to end it (Bancroft, 1998, par. 9).

- Then there was also the love-hate relationship between King David and his son Absalom. There were some family issues going on to which Absalom was not too pleased with the way his dad handled the issue. Apparently one of David's sons named Amnon raped his sister Tamar.

2 Samuel 13:11-14 says "And when she had brought them unto him to eat, he took hold of her, and said unto her, 'come lie with me, my sister'. And she answered him 'Nay, my brother, do not force me, for no such thing ought to be done in Israel; do not thou this folly. And I, whither shall I cause my shame to go? And as for thee, thou shalt be as one of the fools in Israel. Now therefore, I pray thee, speak unto the king; for he will not without me from thee. Howbeit he would not harken unto her voice; but, being stronger than she, forced her, and lay with her (KJV).

- One would assume that family counseling and other forms of intervention would be the reasonable way to go; but instead, Absalom took the law in his hand and killed his brother. He later decided that his father must also die, so he spent many years pursuing his dad in order to kill him and take over his kingdom. 2 Samuel 15:12-14 says

And Absalom sent for Ahithophel the Gilonite, David's counsellor, from his city, even from Giloh, while he offered sacrifices. And the conspiracy was strong; for the people increased continually with Absalom. And there came a messenger to David, saying, The hearts of the men of Israel are after Absalom. And David said unto all his servants that were with him at Jerusalem, Arise, and let us flee; for we shall not else escape from Absalom: make speed to depart, lest he overtake us suddenly, and bring evil upon us, and smite the city with the edge of the sword. (KJV).

After making his attempts to kill his father David, Absalom was later killed during his pursuit to end David's reign and his life. Seeing that domestic violence is so common, yet so hidden in the churches, I believe that Christians, especially those in authority should be trained on how to deal with, and help the victims. It is hard for an abused person to function in the church, it is also very difficult for them to sit and listen to the pastor teach about the love of God, only to be domestically abused later at home. I sat in several churches, and observed them lay their hands on the sick in order to heal them; I also watched pastors spoke ' in tongues' and foamed at the mouth as they ministered to the congregation, and when the dust settled, they returned to their abusive ways. This is bad especially if the victim's spouse is the pastor.

As a result of several interviews, spouses of pastors and other religious leaders complained of physical violence in their homes. They described how fearful they are of their abusers, and as a result are disinclined to inform the authorities. Some confided in me that they are even afraid, and sometimes embarrassed to tell their family members.

There is no way that the love of God can be demonstrated in the church. There is no way that the church can minister to those outside the church. They would probably be better off living their worldly lifestyles where the bad things happen to them as they expected. I respect someone who is a sinner and accept that fact, than one who claims to be a Christian and living sinful lives in secret. Don't they realize that the Lord sees them? and will judge them for their actions? This is certainly not the way that the Lord intended. According to John 3:16 "For God so loved the world, that he gave his only begotten Son, that whosoever believeth in him should not perish, but have everlasting life" (KJV). God loved us so much that He was willing to sacrifice His only Son. If that's not love, then I don't know the full meaning of love.

The church is held to a high standard so that we can effectively reach the world. If we're not right, how can we teach others to get right? These are the actions of hypocrites, and for those of us who are embracing this double-standard, that's exactly what we are. The Merriam-Webster dictionary describes such individual as "a person who claims or pretends to have certain beliefs about what is right but who behaves in a way that disagrees with those beliefs"

Some men love to quote the scriptures in Ephesians 5:22-24 which states "Wives, submit yourselves unto your own husbands, as unto the Lord. For the husband is the head of the wife, even as Christ is the head of the church: and he is the saviour of the body" Therefore as the church is subject unto Christ, so let the wives be to their own husbands in everything (KJV).

However they fail to read further, which included a message for them also. Verses 25-27 also says "Husbands, love your wives, even as Christ also loved the church, and gave himself for it; That he might sanctify and cleanse it with the washing of water by the word, That he might present it to himself a glorious church, not having spot, or wrinkle, or any such thing; but that it should be holy and without blemish" (KJV). Christ not only spoke of His love for the church, He demonstrated His love by dying on the cross for us. He also reached out to those who are rejected by others, as well as the poor and needy. He expected the husband to demonstrate his love for his wife by covering her in prayer, giving himself up for her and becoming one flesh with her.

So obviously Christ is not pleased when His people (whether men or women) ignore His commands and instructions to us, and choose to do things our own way. We cannot choose to live for Christ and the world simultaneously. A choice must be made, just as the scripture says "No man can serve two masters: for either he will hate the one, and love the other; or else he will hold to the one, and despise the other. Ye cannot serve God and mammon." (Matthew 6:24, KJV).

CHAPTER 11

Some Signs of a Domestic Abuser

1. The abuser gives the abused no control over money or any financial issues in the homes.
2. The abuser is constantly criticizing the victim's ways of dressing, or ways of speaking.
3. The abuser usually makes fun of the way the abused eats.
4. Threats to take away the victim's children.
5. Display violence –choking, shouting, shoving, hitting.
6. Teasing the abused in hurtful ways.
7. Embarrassing the victim, belittling him or her in public.
8. A very controlling abuser.
9. The abuser always completes the victim's sentences, or frequently try to speak on his or her behalf.
10. The abuser hates to see the victim shows signs of happiness.
11. Wants to know the victim's whereabouts at all times.
12. The abuser does not claim responsibility for his or her actions. Never apologizes.
13. The abuser can be very charming to everyone, except to the abused.

14. The abuser grew up in abusive violent homes.

15. Indulging in name-callings such as fat, ugly, stupid, dumb, etc.

16. The abuser is the decision maker on all matters in the home.

17. The abuser decides what the victim should wear, what to eat, and where the victim can or cannot go.

18. The abuser prevents the abused from associating with anyone.

19. The abused is constantly coerced by the abuser.

20. The abused person can never do enough to satisfy the abuser.

21. H/she will hurt the other and then says it is the victim's fault.

22. When things are going well, the abuser usually takes the credit. When things are going bad, the victim gets the blame.

CHAPTER 12

Some Subtl Signs to Look Out For

1. An abuser will make you feel like you cannot make it without him/her. He or she will drain you of your self-esteem, and usually do a very good job at it.

2. When an abuser is through with abusing you, the desire to live diminishes greatly because you are made to feel worthless.

3. The unkind words of an abuser are repeated so many times in the homes that after a while, the abused individual starts believing.

4. Many times the abusive person will do his or her deeds behind closed doors so that no one would know, or even believe. "Since this behavior is almost always done behind closed doors, bringing disgrace to both victim and offender, an actual count of the incidence and prevalence of domestic violence is impossible to determine" (Feder, L., 1999. p. 1961).

5. It's important in the case of physical, or any kinds of abuse to know that God detests the abuser's cowardly

actions. Colossians 3:19 says "Husbands, love your wives and do not be harsh with them" (NIV).

1 Peter 3:7 says "In the same way, you husbands must give honor to your wives. Treat her with understanding as you live together. She may be weaker than you are, but she is your equal partner in God's gift of new life. If you don't treat her as you should, your prayers will not be heard" (NIV).

James 1:19-20 also says "So then, my beloved brethren, let every man be swift to hear, slow to speak, slow to wrath; for the wrath of man does not produce the righteousness of God" (NIV).

6. Don't believe an abuser when he/she blames you for his/her anger and violent behavior.
7. Do not try to make yourself unhappy in order to please your partner. The day when you will experience happiness with him/her will never come.
8. Do not lie in order to cover up your spouse's abuse.
9. If your spouse abuses you constantly, and then apologizes to you each time he/she abuses you, beware. Don't believe him/her.

CHAPTER 13

How to Support Someone Who is Being Abused

1. Be there for the individual, be a good listener.
2. Don't judge him/her, or get mad if the person refused to leave the abusive home as you requested.
3. Listen more to the victim, talk less.
4. Do not impose your opinions on him or her.
5. Be certain to let the abused know that no one deserves to be mishandled or exploited.
6. Do not tell others (except the authorities) what the abused victim confides in you. It's important to give him/her the opportunity to tell his/her story.
7. Document everything discussed, including pictures of wounds sustained by the victim.
8. Encourage the abused to seek help.
9. Direct the victim to the nearest shelter.
10. Help the abused to locate all the resources and different organizations available to help her/him to start the recovery process.

11. Don't hesitate to offer help, it may save a life.

12. Remind the abused constantly that it is not his/her fault.

13. Try not to side with either partner, but instead have an open mind. "The worst thing you can do is take sides, even if one party is dead wrong. You don't help by screaming. You can't solve their problems. You just try to calm them down" (Straus, M., Gelles, R., Steinmetz, S., 2006, p. 17).

14. Don't negatively criticize the victim. They last thing an abused person wants to hear is someone speaking ill about them.

Domestic abuse isn't something women share easily because of the shame, guilt and embarrassment that often surround a victim's past. Years ago, I recall opening up to a friend about my own experience, only to have her respond in disgust "And why were you with a guy like that?" Her reaction made me feel stupid for ever having dated him to begin with, and even more foolish for staying with him as long as I had. It also discouraged me from sharing my experience with anyone else who know me, for fear of appearing naïve, flawed, or even masochistic. It took me a long time to realize that the shame was not on me but on him and on anyone who judges a woman for accidentally walking into a nightmare while trying to find a loving relationship. (Fairweather, L., 2012, p. 15).

The most important this is to remember how much God loves and cares for us, and He did not intend for anyone to abuse us physically or otherwise. A few scriptures substantiate that:

- Psalm 11:5 The LORD trieth the righteous: but the wicked and him that loveth violence his soul hateth "(KJV).
- Colossians 3:19 "Husbands, love your wives, and be not bitter against them "(KJV).

1 Corinthians 13:4-7 "Charity suffereth long, and is kind; charity envieth not; charity vaunteth not itself, is not puffed up, Doth not behave itself unseemly, seeketh not her own, is not easily provoked, thinketh no evil; Rejoiceth not in iniquity, but rejoiceth in the truth; Beareth all things, believeth all things, hopeth all things, endureth all things" (KJV).

James 1:19-20 "Wherefore, my beloved brethren, let every man be swift to hear, slow to speak, slow to wrath: For the wrath of man worketh not the righteousness of God" (KJV).

John 13:34 "A new commandment I give unto you, That ye love one another; as I have loved you, that ye also love one another. By this shall all men know that ye are my disciples, if ye have love one to another" (KJV).

Since we know something more about domestic violence and the damage that it can produce, it's now up to us to teach others about its danger. We are also aware of the many ways to avoid this demon. According to Richard Davis,

> Many of us continue to refuse any display of empathy or compassion for the victim of domestic violence until that same calamity strikes one of our own family members or until a friend becomes an abuser or a victim. If we continue to wait for a personal family experience before we become believers, the visit of a domestic violence to a family member or friend will be as inevitable as the visit of the Grim Reaper (Davis, 1998, p.3).

Let us not be silent anymore but instead make our voices heard everywhere. It is a fact that many men are also being abused by women every day, even though women sometimes endure more physical damage. The men sometimes failed to report these incidents for various reasons, one being feelings of embarrassment. Another reason could be that many people (include the authorities) would probably not believe them or take their claims seriously. It doesn't matter the sex of the individual, either way, any kind of abuse is still considered to be abuse, and it is still wrong.

> The violence was not limited to men. Pre-divorce women were almost as violent; they threw objects, scratched, hit, and kicked. But, of course, a 115 or 120 pound woman's blows are not as destructive as a 170 or 200 pound males. Men used some of the same techniques as women, but

angry men were more likely to punch, twist limbs, slam a spouse against a wall, or throw her across a room (Hetherington, E., Kelly, J., 2003, p. 37-38)

I am writing about my experience as a woman just as I experienced it, so if you are abused, regardless of your gender, skin color, culture, or social status, it is wrong, illegal, and not to be tolerated, therefore it must be reported. So, as concerned and caring citizens of this world, let us speak up, speak out and help someone. Who knows, we could be saving lives.

CHAPTER 14

Signs of An Abused Individual

1. The victim is always dressed in long sleeves, and wears dark glasses in order to cover up any scars, or black- eyes from the beatings.
2. He/she always seems withdrawn.
3. Refuses to make any form of eye contact.
4. Shies away from any opportunities to mingle with others.
5. Frequent visits to the emergency room.
6. Frequent suicide attempts.
7. The victim has burns in unusual places.
8. Shows signs of depression and anxiety.
9. Does not like to engage in conversations.
10. Always likes to remain inconspicuous in the background.

Remember that not all abuse involves hitting, so the absence of physical scars does not indicate that there is no abuse. Knowing the signs can alert many victims to the many signals sent by these abusers. "Leading advocacy groups for victims of domestic violence claims that more than half of married women (about 27 million) are beaten by men during their marriage and that more than one-third of married women (18 million women) are battered repeatedly" (Davis, R., 1998, p.3). It's about time that we stop being victims, and lower the number of people being abused each year.

CHAPTER 15

How to Get Help

Thankfully, in today's society there are many different programs available to help the victims of domestic abuse, and also to help the abusers. I did not receive help because I did not know how to get help. "Acknowledging that you were hurt, describing the hurt, and telling its full story is a vital element of the healing process" (Simon, S., Simon, S). Moreover many people were not aware that I was being abused because I tried to hide it. I did not believe that anyone would take the time to listen to me, and I didn't think they would believe me.

There are numerous organizations and shelters that are set up to help with the different issues. There are also resources available to help the victims, as many people are contributing to the cause daily.

In an effort to escape abusive relationships, women rely on a variety of social network, including family and friends, battered women's shelters, domestic violence hotlines, social services and justice systems. Some victims turn to religion and religious institutions in search of refuge, social support, and spiritual guidance to alleviate pain and suffering (Ross, L., 2005, p. 139).

Regardless, getting out of such terrible and dangerous situation is never easy. There is always the fear that the abuser will find and hurt the victim again. They sometimes believe that the authorities will not help the way they are supposed to help the victims. Many times, after an arrest the abuser is allowed to return to the home, which usually lead to more abuse. "When women are victimized by people they know, 18 percent do not report the violent victimization to police because they are afraid of worse violence from the abuser" (Brown, L., McKeon, Duau, F., 1997, p. 8). There is also the fear of losing one's life if the decision is made to leave the home; or even attempt to return home.

Many are abused in this world; but will walk around as if all is well. They put on fake smiles, while hurting and feeling afraid inside. They are either too embarrassed, ashamed or frightened to tell anyone what's going on. They suffer in silence for many reasons while feeling hopeless, confused and lost. Many don't know which way to turn, and it's exactly how their abusers want them to feel (Gates, C., 2010, p. 73).

I experienced those mixed feelings back then, which was why I was so reluctant to leave. I was scared for my life and the lives of my children. It is not easy to walk away especially when I had nowhere to go, no friends and no money. At that time I began to experience several kinds of emotions, some of which were confusion and fear. One minute I thought that I had everything under control, and the next minute I became confused and discontented. And before I realized it, I was right back where I started. Anne Weatherholt explained "After a time, the victim is emotionally exhausted and detaches psychologically. The abuser, sensing the retreat is more controlling and possessive, and monitors the victim's every move" (Weatherholt, 2008, p. 8). The whole experience was a very painful one, I'm not referring to the pain one experiences when they have a stomach or head ache; it is the kind of pain where you cannot describe. But one thing I can tell those of you who are reading this; that it hurts. It is a very painful experience which usually leave many emotional and most times physical scars.

> When family members have been hurt to the core of their being, they are in pain. Such pain has a far reaching impact on the life of the family and if not addressed may continue from one generation to the next in even greater tragic scenarios (Balswick, J., Balswick, B., 2007, p. 294).

It does not matter how wonderful and glamorous one's life may seem, once there is abuse of any kind, it is important to leave. Many times we tell ourselves that we will wait and see if things will get better, but that is not the right thing to do because without help, things will not get better, and you may never leave alive.

If you or anyone you know is being abused, talk to someone you or your friend can trust — a family member, a trusted teacher, a pastor, a doctor, or a school or religious youth counselor. Many teachers and counselors have training in how to recognize and report abuse (DuPont, A., 2011, par. 2).

- Telephone and online directories list local abuse and violence hotline:
- Violence Against Women
- Common Ground: A victim assistance program which advocates for victims of crime, domestic and sexual abuse, and workplace violence.
- Help Guide: A nonprofit organization which help to provide help for abused and battered women. Helpguide. org. 1800-799-7233 (SAFE).

Offers: Legal help, counseling. Support groups. "Of course no support group can fix your life, but it can provide you with the support and understanding you need to ge through the process without losing your sanity along with the way your support group will also provide you with a good dose of reality checks in times when you're not sure that you haven't already lost your mind" (Covy, K., 2006, p. 167).

They also provide services for children; employment programs, health – related services, education opportunities, and financial assistance.

- National Domestic Violence Helpline

  "The National Domestic Violence Hotline (1800-799-SAFE (7233) or TTY 1800-787-3224) provides 24-hour support by offering advocacy, safety planning, resources and hope to everyone affected by domestic violence" (Skaine, R., 2015, p. 198).

- There are also the churches who are always willing to offer solutions for battered spouses. Speak to the pastor of your home church, who will lead you in the right direction.
- Do not be afraid to call 911.

  Most battered women have a difficult time seeking help. Studies and surveys over the past 20 years have found that they travel diverse paths out of abusive relationships. Many battered women are isolated from friends and family and think they have no one close to whom they can turn. Some do turn to family and friends only to be rebuffed, not listened to, or told that need to keep trying for the sake of their marriage, their children, their religion, their extended family or the community (McCue, M., 2008, p. 53).

As a then stranger to this country and not familiar with the laws of this land, I received several advice from many people, all of which sounded great but none worked for me. I was told by an official that I could not leave the home or else I could be charged with abandoning the marital home. I immediately replied "What about the senseless beatings I'm receiving?" I displayed several of my scars, probably to gain sympathy. I was informed that my husband could easily file for divorce due to abandonment and not only would he win the case against me, but I would also lose my children. At the mention of losing my boys, I decided to stay in the home. I began to console myself:

'So what if he hit me again? I made it this far'

'The first few years were hard, but I survived, it will be okay"

"I'll do anything for my children; I cannot imagine my life without them"

"He'd probably take them to some far places where I won't be able to see them again"

These and many other confusing thoughts went through my mind. I want you to see how easy it is for someone in this situation to think and act irrationally. It is also very easy for others who are not in this situation to negatively criticize the individual being abused. Previously I had no tolerance for those who are being domestically abused, because I thought to myself 'Why won't they walk away?' As a result of my horrifying experience, I understand how difficult it is just to walk away.

Today, although it is still a very difficult decision to make, please make the judgement to get help. People are more determined today to break the cycle, so many victims are alerting the authorities as well as the media in order that their voices can be heard. Don't give your abuser another chance to violate you again, because chances are it may be the last chance you'll ever get. Cherry Gates says "Abusers know they have the upper hand when this happens. Normally many will quickly abuse again, which may possibly be more aggressive than before. Get out of abuse relationships, because they're draining, unhealthy and could cause one their life" (Gates, 2010, p.72).

CHAPTER 16

Looking Back Then, What Would I Have Done Differently?

Many years ago, I never thought of domestic abuse because it was very rarely mentioned. Even when I began to realize its existence, I never give the issue a second thought. That is why when I began to experience its effects, I was so surprised, because I've never seen it in action. Even after I escaped the claws of abuse, it was not my intention to talk about it, in fact I tried to bury it. Thank God for giving me the ability to talk about it so others can hear. I am grateful for all the wonderful people who the Lord placed in my company to give me the courage and the strength to make this book a reality, which will be helpful to many, many hurting people

Looking back into my years as an abused wife, I realized that there were some things I would have done differently. For one thing I wouldn't live with an abuser; as soon as signs of the abuse surfaced I would definitely relocate without giving it a thought as to where I would live. The problem was that after sometime I became quite comfortable with the violence, believing that I would become immune to it, or he would probably get tired of hitting me and decide to stop. In fact it got much worse. I began to convince myself that it wasn't all that bad. "I didn't leave because I grew accustomed to living a lie. He never pushed, tripped or slapped me in public. He was generally careful to train his taunts and gibes so they appeared to be nothing more than innocuous teasing" (Weiss, E., 2000, p. 23).

As I write this book, I realized how close I came to losing my life at the hands of my abuser. I kept giving him chance after chance because I was hoping that he would change. I also felt sorry for him (and probably still love him) that is why I never tried to get him arrested. In a weird way I thought that he loved me in spite of the violence. As a matter of fact I thought that by being supportive, I could change him. This is one of the biggest mistakes that are made by the victims. No matter what we try to do in order to make situations better, it will not work. It might appear that things are working out, but it is only for a short while. In my situation I used to tread lightly, so to speak, just so I wouldn't upset him. I remembered on some occasions the idea worked well but only for a while, and whenever he decided to become angry again it was always worse than before. It was like he was taking two steps forward and six steps backward.

Another thing I would do differently would to alert the authorities as many times as it would take, because I feared that the police would come to the house and find no reason to take action; after they leave I would be abused all over again. I figured if I make numerous reports, after a while they would definitely believe me. I also thought that if he should be arrested and later released, it would make matters worse for me, because for one thing he would evict me from the home, and I wouldn't be able to care for myself and the children. These are some of the issues that the victims face every day, which explains why it is not easy for them to suddenly get up and leave without any sense of planning or direction. In today's age, I would do everything in my power to make my abuse public. This would include taking lots of pictures and careful documentation.

I would definitely encourage my partner to seek professional help because it was quite obvious that he needed help. It was noticeable that he had anger issues by the way he lashed out in anger so frequently. I certainly would not walk away from him in that manner. I would leave for sure but not without suggesting to him, or others that he needs some form of intervention.

I would make every effort to shield the children from witnessing such horrible acts of abuse. One of my biggest fears was that the effects of the abuse would have negative impact on them. I was also fearful that I would lose my standing as a good parent to them if I abandon the home and having nowhere else to go. "In different type of scenario many spouses are afraid of losing a certain lifestyle. Their fear drags them back under the sheets of abusive relationships. Without their ever trying to help the abuser change" (Lamm, B., 2009, n.p).

Looking back there are numerous lessons learned, one very important one is that domestic, spiritual, emotional, and other kinds of abuse are no respecters of persons. Even God's children experienced their effects. As a result of my interviews, many are still living the destructive life at this very moment. "Believers are certainly not exempt from committing physical violence"

(Nason-Clarke, N., Clark-Kroger, C., Fisher-Townsend, B., 2011, p. 36). I applaud the church leaders who are dealing with this problem in their churches. Joycelyn Anderson says "The Christian woman whose spirit is being crushed and whose life is endangered by domestic violence needs straight answers – not unrealistic expectations or clichéd, stereotypical platitudes" (Anderson, 2007, p. 15).

Another lesson I learned is that I should not assume that once an individual escape a dangerous situation, it does not mean that the victim's ordeal is over. For many, it is just the beginning as the after-effects are sometimes far worse.

> Those who have never experienced an abusive or violent relationship often believe that once survivors find their way out, all difficulties are solved, life is good, they are safe, and recovery will be swift. But survivors soon learn that leaving in itself is not the end of the nightmare. It is the beginning of a difficult, yet fulfilling and rewarding journey toward healing and happiness (Dugan, M., Hook, R.).

When we refuse or are afraid to take action and seek help, everyone is affected as a result. The victim suffers greatly, also the family and subsequently society. According to Kristin Anne Kelly

> As domestic violence becomes more visible, the enormous price it exacts from all members of society is increasingly clear. The annual monetary cost of battering, including

medical coverage, workdays missed, and consumption of valuable legal and social resources, is estimated to be in the billions. But perhaps even more noteworthy are the costs incurred when a generation of children who witness and are often the recipients of brutal treatment, learn to view violence as normal (Kelly/ 2003, p. 1).

Conclusion

This book was not only written for victims of domestic violence, instead it was written also for the families of those who are experiencing this abuse. Also our close friends or neighbors who are currently living this kind of ill treatment. It is also written for those who think it's okay to mistreat or misuse God's beautiful people; it is to tell you to stop now. Remember that God did not create us to be someone else's punching bags, but instead to love and cherished. 1 John 4:7 says "Beloved, let us love one another: for love is of God; and every one that loveth is born of God, and knoweth God" (KJV).

Mark 12:30 also says "And thou shalt love the Lord thy God with all thy heart, and with all thy soul, and with all thy mind, and with all thy strength: this is the first commandment" (KJV). Ephesians 5:33 states "And thou shalt love the Lord thy God with all thy heart, and with all thy soul, and with all thy mind, and with all thy strength: this is the first commandment" (KJV).

Lynn Wingert says,

> Domestic violence happened in all sorts of homes in the Victorian era, both rich and poor, and the violence took a number of different forms. It was not limited to physical

beatings. Domestic violence was – and continues to be – an equal opportunity bully (Wingert, 2001, p. 4).

It does not matter who we are: man, woman, boy or girl, we must be able to live with, and love each other the way God love us. Many children witnessed the abusive pattern in the homes and grow up thinking that it is okay to act in similar ways to their spouses. They also grow up expecting to be abused because they lived it and believed it is okay to be violated.

Growing up in a family where there is violence or abuse can make a person think that is the right way or the only way for family members to treat each other. Somebody who has only known an abusive relationship might mistakenly think that hitting, beating, pushing, shoving, or angry name-calling are perfectly normal ways to treat someone when you're mad (DuPont, A., 2014, par. 2).

Tony Gaskins Jr. says in his mobile upload "Ladies hear this. If a man isn't following God, he isn't fit to lead. If he doesn't have a relationship with God, he won't know how to have a relationship with you. If he doesn't know God, he doesn't know real love" (Gaskins). We must also learn the art of loving and respecting one another. It's the only way that we can move on and function properly in society. Nothing hinders an individual from progressing more than when he/she is being demeaned and depreciated on a constant basis. The experience is usually unforgettable for many and pay have lasting effects. In order to prevent this from happening, it's important for us to share our stories any way we can, so that others will be aware of its existence, and the abused can be helped. Hillary Abrahams says:

> I will not wreck this experience. I have to make something good out of it. Otherwise I suffered for no reason....and that....that's not acceptable to me. I've got scars on my face....yeah, I can't waste the experience, I do have to do something with it....so I have to share anything that could be put to use for other people (Abrahams, H., 2010, p. 15).

We must get into the habit of speaking out, the longer we suffer in silence, the worse our situations will get. The scripture is in favor of us sharing our stories or testimonies. As Edward Everett Hale said in one of his many quotes, "I am only one. But I am one. I cannot do everything, but I can do something. And I will not let what I cannot do interfere with what I can do" So as Christian men and women of this beautiful world, let's help someone by speaking out.

I pray God's blessing upon you and your family as you go through the difficult healing process. However long it takes, do not turn or look back, but instead keep going forward. There will be some days where you feel like you cannot go on any longer, but call on someone you trust, who can give you words of encouragement and to also pray with you. Also pray every day for God's strength because this process is a daily walk. Relief will not happen overnight, but for every day that you persevere, you're one step closer to your recovery. As a survivor, for over twenty years,

I still experience my 'down' days, but I trust in God to see me through my step each day. Always remember that you are never alone. God loves you, and I love you too.

REFLECTION QUESTIONS

1. What are some of the red flags that alert you to the fact someone is a domestic abuser?

_____

_____

_____

_____

_____

2. If you are living next door to a home where a spouse is constantly being abused. Do you think it's okay to ignore the violence?

_____

_____

_____

_____

_____

3. Would you report an abuser who is a very close family member?

_____

_____

_____

_____

_____

4. If not, please explain why

_____

_____

_____

_____

_____

5. Growing up I recalled many times my family became aware of domestic issues among the neighbors, but was always told to 'stay out of other people's business' Do you think this is the right thing to do?

_____

_____

_____

_____

_____

6. Prior to my experience with domestic violence, I used to make statements such as "Why does she stay to be beaten over and over? All she had to do is leave'. Do you think these are fair statements?

_____

_____

_____

_____

_____

7. If you do, why?

_____

_____

_____

_____

8. If not, why?

_____

_____

_____

_____

9. Were you ever a victim of domestic violence?

_____

_____

_____

_____

_____

10. If so, are you currently in such situation?

_____

_____

_____

_____

11. If you were in the past, how did you survive?

_____

_____

_____

_____

12. What would you do if you suspect that your very close friend is being abused?

_____

_____

_____

_____

13. Does your abusive partner make you feel guilty each time he/she abuses you?

_____

_____

_____

_____

_____

14. Each time my partner hit me, I used to blame it on his stressful job. Can you relate to this way of thinking?

_____

_____

_____

_____

_____

If you are currently being abused by your spouse or anyone else in your home, you must make the decision to leave immediately and call for help. You must leave, seek shelter and dial 911. Also if you know of anyone who is living in abusive situations, don't dismiss it, it is much your concern as the individual who is being violated. Speak up, tell someone in authority and get help for that person. Be concerned about the cruelty that others are enduring, the next victim could be one of your family members, or it could happen to you.

Let us be our brother's keeper.

Proverbs 27:12 "A prudent man foreseeth the evil, and hideth himself; but the simple pass on, and are punished." (KJV).

Psalm 143:9 "Deliver me, O LORD, from mine enemies: I flee unto thee to hide me" (KJV).

Sources

Abrahams, H., *Rebuilding Lives After Domestic Violence: Understanding Long-Term Outcomes.* Jessica Kingsley Publishers. Philadelphia, PA. (2010).

Anderson, J., *Woman Submit! Christians and Domestic Violence.* One Way Café Press. Auburndale, FL. (2007).

Balswick, B, Balswick, B., *The Family.* Baker Academic. Grand Rapids, MI. (2007).

Bancroft, L., Retrieved on 5/31/2015 from http://www. lundybancroft.com/articles/understanding-the-batterer-in-custody-and-visitation-disputes (1998).

Bancroft, L., *Why Does He Do That? : Inside the Minds of Angry and Controlling Men.* The Berkley Publishing Group. New York, NY (2002).

Bettino, C., *Directions: Your Roadmap to Happiness.* Dog Ear Publishing. Indianapolis, IN. (2009).

Bishop, E-dee., *God's Antidote for Poisoned Emotions.* Xlibris Corporation. Bloomington, IN> (2009).

Brown. L., McKeon, M., Duau, F., *Stop Domestic Violence.* St. Martin's Press. New York, NY. (1997).

Buzawa, E., Buzawa, C., *Domestic Violence: The Criminal Justice Response.* Sage Publishers. Thousand Oaks, CA. (2003).

Chapman, G., *Desperate Marriages.* Northfield Publishing. Chicago, IL (2008).

Cobb, C., *An Abusive Relationship.* The Rosen Publishing Group, Inc. New York. NY. (2001).

Colson, M., *Coping with Domestic Violence.* Capstone Global Library. North Mankato, MN. (2011).

Covy, K., *When happily Ever After Ends: How to Survive Your Divore Emotionally, Financially and Legally.* Sphinx Publishers. Naperville. IL.

Crisp, K., *He Loves Me, He Loves Me Not.* Xulon Press. Maitland, FL. (2010).

Davis, R. *Domestic Violence, Facts and Fallacies.* Praeger Publishers. Westport, CT. (1998).

Dugan, M., Hock, D., *It's My Life Now: Starting Over After An Abusive Relationship or Domestic Violence.* Routledge, New York. NY. (2006).

DuPont, A., Retrieved on 11/25/2014 from http://kidshealth.org/teen/your_mind/families/family_abuse.html# (2014).

Evans, P., *Victory over Verbal Abuse: A Healthy Guide to Renewing Your Spirit and Reclaiming Your Life.* Adams Media. Avon, MA. (2012).

Fairweather, L., *Stop Signs: Recognizing, Avoiding, and Escaping Abusive Relationships.* Seal Press. Berkley, CA. (2012).

Feder, L., *Women and Domestic Violence: An Interdisciplinary Approach.* The Haworth Press, Inc. Binghamton, NY. (1999).

Formica, M., Retrieved on 5/29/2015 fromhttps://www.psychologytoday.com/blog/enlightened-living/200807/understanding-the-dynamics-abusive-relationships (2014).

Gates, C., *People Lie, But the Signs Don't.* Lulu Publishers. Raleigh, NC. (2010).

Goldberg, J., Retrieved on 7/01/2015 from http://www.webmd.com/balance/stress-management/effects-of-stress-on-your-body. (2014).

Hale, E., Retrieved on 8/12/2015 from https://en.wikiquote.org/wiki/Edward_Everett_Hale (2015).

Hart, A., *Adrenaline and Stress: The Exciting New Breakthrough That Helps You Overcome Stress Damage.* Thomas Nelson Publishers. Nashville, TN.

Hanmer, J., Itzin, C., *Home Truths about Domestic Violence.* Routledge, New York, NY. (2000).

Harne, L., Radford, J., *Tackling Domestic Violence: Theories, Policies and Practice.* Open University Press. New York, NY. (2008).

Hetherington, E., Kelly, J., *For Better or for Worse: Divorce Reconsidered.* W.W. Morton & Company Inc. New York, NY. (2003).

Howard, L., Feder, G., Agnew-Davies, R., *Domestic Violence and Mental Health.* RC Psych Publications. Belgrave Square, London. (2013).

Howell, C., *The Simple Life.* Xlibris Publishing. Bloomington, IN. (2011).

Kelly, K., *Domestic Violence and the Politics of Privacy.* Cornell University Press. Ithaca, NY. (2003).

Kroeger, C., Nason-Clark, *No Place for Abuse: Biblical & Practical Resources to Counteract Domestic Violence.* InterVarsity Press. Downers Grove, IL. (2001).

Lamm, B., *How to Help the One You Love.* Martin's Press, New York, NY. (2009).

McCue, M., *Domestic Violence: A Reflection Handbook.* ABC-CL1O, Inc., Santa Barbara, CA. (2008).

Murray, S., Gelles, R., Steinmetz, S., *Behind Closed Doors: Violence in the American Family.* Transaction Publishers. Vanwick, NJ. (2006).

Parrott, L., *Shoulda, Coulda, Woulda: Live in the present, Find your Future.* Zondervan. Grand Rapids, MI. (2003).

Ross, L., *Continuing the War Against Domestic Violence.* Taylor and Francis Group. Boca Raton, Fl. (2005).

Sells, J., Yarhouse, M., *Counseling Couples in Conflict.* InterVarsity Press. Downers Grove, IL. (2011).

Schaefer, A., *Staying Healthy.* Capstone Capital Library, LLC. Chicago, ILL (2010).

Shields, A. (2006) (Reconciled to Violence: State Failure to Stop Domestic Abuse and Abduction). Human Rights Watch,

18 (9). Retrieved from https://books.google.com/books?id= mcVSdoZEjwwC&dq=Perpetrators+of+domestic+violence+ variously...A.+Shields&q=copyright#v=onepage&q=copyright &f=false.

Shipway, L., *Domestic Violence: A Handbook for Health Professionals.* Outledge. New York, NY. (2004).

Simon, S, Simon, S., *Forgiveness.* Warner Books, New York, NY. (1990).

Skaine, R., *Abuse: An Encyclopedia of causes: Consequences and Treatments.* Greenwood. Santa Barbara, CA. (2015).

Thomas, G., *Sacred Marriage.* Zondervan. Grand Rapids, MI. (2000).

Weatherholt, A., *Breaking the Silence: The Church Responds to Domestic Violence.* (2008).

Weinstein, R., *The Stress Effect.* The Penguin Group. New York, NY. (2004).

Weiss, E., *Surviving Domestic Violence: Voices of Women Who Broke Free.* Agreka Books. Sandy, UT.

Wilson, K., *When Violence Begins at Home.* Hunter House Publications. Alameda, CA. (2006).

Wingert, L., *Battered, Bruised and Abused Women: Domestic Violence in Nineteenth Century.* Pro Quest. Ann Arbor, MI. (2001).

Woulas, M., *The Ticking Time Bomb.* Lulu Publishing & Lattitude Media. Raleigh, NC. (2010).

About the author

Yvonne Maxine Weir (born Yvonne Maxine Davis) was born on August 8, to Melbourne and Edith Davis in the beautiful island of Jamaica. There she attended three of the best schools in the island: Park Hall Primary School in Park Hall, Frankfield High School in Frankfield, and Clarendon College, located in Chapelton. After graduating from high school, she enrolled in the nursing program for some years until 1980, when her son and her immigrated to the United States. She lived in New Jersey for several years before moving to sunny Florida, where she continued her nursing profession. After the birth of her daughter, she decided to start her own business; that way she could bond with her children while simultaneously earning a living. She owned and operated the Little League Day Care Center for several years, which she later traded for her income tax and financial business which is still operating today.

During that time, she realized that her children were experiencing separation anxiety in school, so she became a volunteer in the public schools to be close to them during school hours. It was while volunteering that she met a very good friend who introduced her to Trinity International University. As a pastor she thought, *What better place to sharpen her pastoral skills than a Christian university?* Not only did she become a more learned woman of God, but her other skills as a writer and poetess were stimulated. The birth of this book, as well as the other books, came about as a result of her enrollment at this university. The teaching and training she received at this school encouraged and inspired her to write several books.

She is currently pastoring at Rehoboth Outreach Center (R. O. C.) in Miami. She is also the founder and president of The Youth for Christ Foundation.

Of all her achievements, her greatest accomplishments are her children: Michael, Linval, Sasha, Carlton Jr. (CJ), Samantha, and Clifford. She thanks God for them and pray that they will prosper in whatever they do

Printed in the United States
By Bookmasters